Hebridean Altars

David Adam Recommends:

Hebridean Altars

The Spirit of an Island Race

Alistair Maclean

Hodder & Stoughton

LONDON SYDNEY AUCKLAND

British Library Cataloguing in Publication Data
A record for this book is available from the British Library

ISBN 0 340 73557 0

Typeset by Avon Dataset Ltd, Bidford-on-Avon, Warks

Printed and bound in Great Britain by
Clays Ltd, St Ives plc

Hodder and Stoughton Ltd
A Division of Hodder Headline PLC
338 Euston Road
London NW1 3BH

Dedicated to
my dear wife

ACKNOWLEDGMENTS

I OWE deep thanks to two dear friends, Donald MacGillivray, the minister of Petty, and Hector Cameron, the minister of Moy. Their encouragements, their suggestive criticism with their instinct for the good word have helped me much. And I am grateful, too, to another friend who read the MS., Dr. Donald J. MacLeod, whose knowledge of Gaelic folklore is unrivalled.

Whoever brings a gentle mind to what is written here, may He bless, who loves us all, and, as they read, may each catch a vision of The One Face.

ALISTAIR MACLEAN

ACKNOWLEDGMENTS

FOREWORD

BY DAVID ADAM, VICAR OF HOLY ISLAND

I am delighted to commend *Hebridean Altars* to new readers. This book has been long out of print and is much sought after. It is a book that has enriched my life and extended my vision of the world and its Creator. Coming across *Hebridean Altars* for the first time was like walking into a new country. Here was a rich landscape, high and majestic peaks, and mighty seas, even the mist filled valleys had a glory to them. Here among the strange enveloping fog burst bright rays of sunshine. It was as if I was suddenly walking out of the mist into a clear and beautiful view that was endless. At the same time, it felt like coming home, for this was the world and the earth that I loved much. What excited me was the sheer delight in the world and in worldly images. I realised this was a world so many of us had lost, yet hungered for and yearned to find. I am sure so many travellers of today are hoping that they will stumble upon such a world. Through reading this book they may just discover the place they are looking for is nearer than they had ever thought possible. For here we become aware that God is at home in our homes, and our prayer can be quite homely.

Alistair Maclean is a poet and only a poet could capture the mysteries that the people of the Hebrides shared with him. Maclean mourns the loss of the ' clan of mystics, & beauty lovers: the finders of happiness: the gentle folk whose wealth is hidden in themselves . . . the women who work hard but have the dawn in their eyes'. Time and again he makes us long to see such a dawn, like in the ' Morning that Makes all Amends'. He does not however run away from the ' cheerless isle' or the ' ebbing of life', rather he sees beyond them: he sees in the depths the power, the glory and the love of God. This may seem a rarefied atmosphere but it is written by a man with his feet firmly on the ground and his ears open to the stories of the ordinary people around him. There is something that is very Celtic in the deep love for the world and for the ordinary, knowing it contains the extra ordinary and the very presence of God. Maclean sees with the eyes of a visionary and invites us to do the same. Through this book my heart was touched with beauty and glory, my eyes were opened and a whole new world view was discovered. The wonderful discovery is that this is God's world and He has not left it, God loves His creation and is ever to be found within it. As God loves His world, we must learn to love it and enjoy it with all our heart.

The Island faith and culture survived the Puritan burning of its music, fiddles and pipes; it survived the clearances, and the forbidding of the use of its own language in schools; it survived the loss of so many of its men in two world wars. It has succumbed to radio and television. What had been handed down by word of mouth for generations, prayers that had been part of the fabric of their lives, stories of valour and folk wisdom – all are being lost to a television culture. A spiritual depth and insight that was natural and gave purpose and joy to many lives is to be lost to the screen and the 'soaps'. A precious spirit is being taken away from the earth, a species threatened with extinction. If we lose such a heritage, and the richness that the past offers to us, we will be poor indeed, and life will be in danger of becoming a great game of trivial pursuits. Some may feel it is like trying to enter a land that time forgot. Let me assure you there are great treasures here, there are insights that will enrich your life forever.

Thank God that Alistair Maclean met with and shared with this Hebridean folk. He captures for us an age that has gone, yet whose thoughts and prayers can pluck at the very strings of our heart and soul. Here is music indeed that will give rhythm to our lives. How suited to our world is the prayer: ' Take me from the tumult of things into Thy presence. There show me what I am and what Thou purposed me to be. Then hide me from Thy tears.' (page 6). Time and again there is a wonderful way of learning to accept the new day as a gift, a mystery and a companioning with God.

Maclean kept in his little note-book traditions, customs, legends and history that he believed would ' illumine and strengthen the Faith': I have no doubt they will do that for anyone who will take the time to allow these reflections and prayers to work.

DAVID ADAM, HOLY ISLAND.

INTRODUCTION

THE HEBRIDEAN

Surely these are the Blessed Isles
In ancient legend, farmed and sung,
Whereto the tired wanderer comes,
A dream 'twixt heaven and ocean hung.

WE sat together, under the shadow of a rock, each of us, in his own way, worshipping the glory that is the Hebrides. Summer was at its noon and, to make perfect harmony of the hour and scene, so was the sun. A wind, soft as canach petal and scented with the attar of the machair flowers, breathed rather than blew across the isle. A West wind to be sure. Now and then, and faintly, we caught the bass of the sea-music, slow and low, like that of a requiem. A moorland lochan, fed by secret springs, drowsed at our feet, three swans motionless upon its cool breast. Above us, and between the blue of the sky and the brown of the earth, floated the wonder veil, the veil of the purple light. Of it the Hebrideans used to tell this story. On the day of the year that was clearest and most still the folk who had come from the Hebrides to the Upper Land leant out over the golden sills and, for the space of an hour, saw everything as it once had been. Their old homes. Little ones at play. Roses blushing in the gardens. Men drinking deep from wayside wells. Lovers with misty eyes wandering through a hazel wood whose other name is Eden. It was a sight, however, that was ill for peace of mind—as things beyond your reach mostly are. So the Good One, who knows what is best for everyone, gave the veil of the purple light to His four archangels, bidding them spread it well between the blue of the sky and the brown of the earth. And this His servitors do. And there is such a depth of purple in it that the Upper Folk cannot see the Isles. And nowadays are well content. ' What the eye does not see,' says the Gaelic proverb, ' the heart will not desire.'

That day, when we both drank our fill from Beauty's chalice, I was a lad in my teens. My companion was a cattle-dealer. He was of Mull. A soft-spoken kind of man. Quick of pride. A treasure-chest of ancient wisdoms and songs and tales. And, to speak sooth, as tender a creature as you would meet in with between dawn and the dark feather of the dusk. But as shrewd as he was kind and as just as he was both—which is the open secret of the prospering man. And, to be sure, John of the Cattle (to give him his by-name) was all that. At least the gossips had it so. His book-learning was small. Often, as he sat at a farm ingle on a winter's night, a mischievous boy, looking up from his exercise book, would ask him with much politeness to multiply nine times seven. John never could remember. ' The seven shames be upon me,' he would sigh, ' but I never could mind that one.' He really knew no language but his own, his English being as laughable as an Englishman's Gaelic. In his own he was a master, so that it was a joy to hear him speak. He had an instinct for the choice word, an instinct which somehow or other made the word inevitable. Like a goldsmith of Amsterdam who fixes on the only possible jewel for a ring or pendant. I must add that his looks belied him. If you had caught sight of him at a cattle-fair in Skye or Uist—that tall lithe body of his and jaunty stride and roving eye—you would have said at once that he was a dealer and thought no more about him. But, that day, if you could have listened to him, as I did, with all a boy's amazement, you would have known that your judgment had been a hasty thing and that you were in the company of a mind and spirit finer by far than your own. I can see him still through the haze of ever-dimming light that lies between fifteen and fifty. And always with a warm thankfulness. Since he it was who taught me that, in his essence, a man is a spirit, and that the essence of spirit is truth and beauty and love. The legend of the veil of the purple light was his story, as was the reason why the King of the Elements made the Hebrides. A fanciful reason, you may urge, and with as much weight in it as thistledown. I agree. Yet the man and the day and the scene gave it such an air of sincerity, not to speak of glamour, that I was clean cast under a spell—so deep a spell and witching that I sometimes think I have not wakened from it yet.

'These islands,' he breathed, with a gesture towards the North, 'aye, 'tis myself that is as fond of them as a mother of her baby-child, and, mind you, they are the great favourites with the Good One above us as well.'

'Indeed,' said I.

'Yes,' he went on, 'or rather, as I should say, the greatest favourites of all. Now,' he raised his forefinger impressively, 'listen to what I am telling you. The Good One made the Hebrides on the eighth day.'

'The eighth day!' I cried, 'but the Bible . . .'

He waved his hand for silence. 'The Bible is a grand book entirely, and the stories of Samson and the other noble heroes in it are warming to the heart. But, mark you, lad, a man who writes a large book cannot mind everything and'—he hummed a little at this point—' and, like enough, the decent man forgot about the Islands being made the eighth day. But they were, and this was the way of it. The world was finished and the Good One was mighty tired and took a rest and, while He was resting, He thought " Well, I have let my earth-children see the power of my mind, in rock and mountain and tree and wind and flower. And I have shown them the likeness of my mind, for I have made theirs like my own. And I have shown them the love of my mind, for I have made them happy. But halt," says the Good One to Himself, " I have not shown them the beauty of my mind." So the next day, and that was the eighth day, He takes up a handful of jewels and opens a window in the sky and throws them down into the sea. And those jewels are the Hebrides. I had the story of it from my father's father,' he went on. ' An extra fine man, and terrible strong for the truth.'

' What did he do,' I asked. ' Oh,' said John, ' a dealer in beasts like myself, a gentleman to the marrow—though he died bare.' He shook his head gloomily. ' It does not do to be too truthful in our trade,' he muttered as he rose and moved away.

Dear John of the Cattle, may you have your share of Paradise! I often think of him, and every

Midsummer's Day, I find myself wondering whether he leans over a heavenly casement, hoping for a weather-gleam in the purple veil and a glimpse of the Isles. In his biography of Beethoven, Richard Specht has one sentence, rich in loveliness and insight, which mirrors for me the portrait of my old friend. ' Some men still remain in whom humility and devotion in the presence of greatness are still alive and to whom existence without exaltation is unbearable.'

FOREGROUND AND BACKGROUND

Now this man was no solitary. He was not rare. Nor unique. Or, as you might imagine, a thrall to fantasy. On the contrary, he was a normal Hebridean and his spirit-brothers were to be met with from The Lewis to Jura. The clan, sorrow be, seems to grow smaller year by year, the clan of the mystics and the beauty-lovers: the tellers of the fine tales: the finders of happiness: the gentle folk whose wealth is hidden in themselves. Although, to be sure, you may light on them still. In ferrymen's houses. In ancient weather-beaten inns which have yielded food and cordial to travelling men throughout the centuries. At dusk, in fishermen's cabins where the grumbling tide or a mother's croon is the only music. Or in farm kitchens where tired eyes stare into the red of the peat and watch a dream go by—there, to this hour, you may foregather with many a fair mind: men and women who work hard, yet have the dawn in their eyes: whose thought has the dew about it and the wind and the snow: whose hospitality is so ungrudging that they have given the word a new meaning: whose inner serenity is a breastplate the spears of change thrust at in vain, and in whose faces you catch the air of one seeking a far country. We are not a wonder race, by any means, we Hebrideans. We lack a score of the virtues which have made the Scot and the Englishman the kings of the world. We are too much thirled to yesterday, the mother of our foolish prides. We have too little valour of will. For all that, there is a quality of spirit in us which does set us apart and which may even show those who go in quest of it how great a thing it is to be a man.

The notes of this spirit are friendliness and faith, never loud, but ever pure and clear. If the Hebridean is no respecter of persons, he is a respecter of spirit and his friendliness is the urge he feels in his own spirit to make contact with yours. His speech, accordingly, is heartspeech. His courtesy he cannot lay aside, since it is the garment of his inner self. So when he says to you under his own roof, ' Good-night. Sweet sleep to you and a sound waking,' or when parting from you at his door, ' Would it not be the lovely thing for me, if you were only coming instead of going,' he means his own beautiful words. How beautiful in their sincerity those of us who are Hebrideans know. Like the kisses of a little child. Like a mother's benediction which follows down the years.

About the Hebridean's faith two things fall to be said. The one is that the core of it is his radiant trust in Another's care. The other that it is coloured and transfigured by the legends, the traditions, and the lives of those Island saints whose name is a name of honour for a king. Even to this day these men haunt the thought and speak through our people's lips. As this tale will tell. Upon a day that was not yesterday nor the day before it, a farmer and his good wife sat together in their kitchen. Their eyes held a hurt for which words are no balm. His hand crushed a letter, a cry of pain from across the seas, from Donald, his son and hers. The velvet of the dusk draped the hills. Donald's wife had left him and her child. The usual sordid reason. With a sudden gesture of loathing the old man threw it in the fire. It flamed up to red, red as his anger, then down to grey, grey as her fate. As he watched it burn, he cursed her with a curse infinitely bitter. But his wife said nothing. Nothing for a time. Then her voice floated across the silence. 'I fear,' she murmured, 'our son did not seek Columba's blessing on his bridal, but this will bring him to the Holy Feet.' Columba's blessing on his bridal! What an electrifying sentence! What a magic wand! It waves, and lo! a door opens, and you look through it and down past the centuries that are dust. And see Iona with the blue of the sea and the white of the sand and the emerald grass—all shimmering in the sun. And the rude cells of holy men. And coracles rocking in the Sound. And the princely one himself, Columba talking with king or chief or vassal who are come for blessing on their ventures. ... Everyone, she meant, reaches the cross-roads of decision. There Columba stands. The symbol he, of the wise tested man, rich in counsels, and knowledgeable of the way that is plain and safe. But if, hot-foot after blind desire, you will not stop to ask it, then alas for you. For, you will choose the way perilous. Of which the end is heart-pain and the secret tear. Still let the love of the good be in you, and the Love Eternal will win you, and you rise again. I had this story given me, four years ago, by a Catholic sailor from the Island of Barra. It moved him as much as it did me. That was utterly.

While faith and friendliness are the ground colours of it, the Hebridean's portrait, to be complete, ought to show the face of an adventurer. Since that is what he and his sister are fated to be. The tragedy of the Islands is that of the countryside as a whole. There is no room. Therefore they must bundle and go. And they do go, and the lave of them do well, being men of their hands and women of a steadfast mind. You will find them in nearly all the professions. Most are quietly successful, a few romantically so. The Lewis, for example—that stern nursing mother of brains and courage—can boast of sons who have made great fortunes: of not a few whose scholarship has added lustre to her fame and to their own: of others, the most numerous of all, who go down to the sea in ships, and, like the Elizabethan sailors, 'find their joy upon the sea-breast.' Wherever they fare, this sense of serenity, which I have tried to describe, goes with them. At all events with those whose spirit keeps its quality. A strange, unshareable secret. As if, whenever they wish to, they may bathe their thought in the Well of Purity. Or step into a garden of Araby where never the wind blows loudly. Or pass through the curtain of mystery that hangs between Here and There, and speak with Truth and Beauty in a sun-lit land.

The American poet, Sarah Teasdale, has a challenging verse in which she cries —
> ' It is all one, the coming or the going
> If I have kept the last essential me.'

A lovely aspiration and—a warfare from which there is no discharge. I have already shown what this ' essential me' of the Island folk actually is. But why it is what it is is another question. Why is the Hebridean what he is or she? What influences have gone to the making of a spirit which finds an equal joy in dreams and deeds? The answer is that they are the influences of simple human things: his intimacies with the brown earth and the trees and the seasons and the high hills and the sea: his response to the magic of old songs and brave tales: his heirship of courage and of those wisdoms which have come down to him in the shape of proverbs and through folk-lore and plant-lore and his loving study of animals. Out of these unseen stories he has built for his thought a fane of strength and grace. There are close on ten thousand proverbs, many in everyday use. And this for the reason that, while the English proverb is something you suddenly remember, the Gaelic proverb is part of your stock of ideas. Sometimes it is your ammunition in argument, and, if you are nimble enough, the sword-stroke that finishes it. The

Gaelic proverb adds a curious literary flavour to ordinary small-talk and the delightful feeling that you are not merely right but right beautifully. Here are a few: ' Grace and haste are steeds that will not run in harness.' It is the first lesson a Highland gentlewoman gives her daughter. ' Whether he fares over sea or land the happy man keeps his treasure aye' (' *Air muir no monadh tha a' chuid fhein aig an duine shona*'). ' I will go tomorrow,' said the King. ' You will wait my will,' said the wind. What a charming way of saying that everyone has a master—even kings! Another subtle one tells you that ' a man is better than men.' It looks mysterious, but is not. Its point is that leadership counts for more than numbers. And still another informs you that ' gentlehood must be kept in good order.' Which is a thrust at whoever fancies that culture and good breeding, however you have come by them, are enough. They are not enough. A gift is lost for lack of exercise.

Legend and fable, the orange-gold threads of Hebridean folk-lore, are so closely knit together that you can hardly tell which is which. Yet each snatches a grace for you beyond the rules of art and reason. This is the charm of that great classic of sea-travel, Martin's *Description of the Western Islands of Scotland*. He made his voyage in or about 1695, and then set down what he saw and what he heard and how he fared, in an English so warm and so pure and so fine that it is joy, without stint, to read him. The wonders he met in with were legion: ' a man who lost his sight at the moon's change': ' a vow he heard made at the eating of a swan': ' a custom for procuring a fair wind': ' how bleeding is staunched by an herb': ' how the carmel-root aromatic prevents drunkenness'—and a hundred more that are nothing, of course, but pure foolishness. But for everyone in whom the child mind lingers, pure delight as well. Now, while the Islesman has quite outgrown his faith in spirits and fairies and sacred wells and dark enchantments, the sense of mystery, which is the air they breathe, still holds him by its strand invisible. I sometimes liken him to one who listens to a violin in a quiet room at dusk. The notes die down to silence. Yet for him the music does not cease. Though another may not catch them, the lovely strains play on and on and on, quivering and rising and falling on his inner ear. It is after this mode that the voices of his storied past echo and re-echo through the chamber of the Gaelic mind. For a while he walks through it bespelled: then, with a sigh, steps into the cold light of a world where he must earn his bread. And the spell is broken. But the mystery and wonder it distils remain.

There was a day, and that was not so long ago, when every Highland woman knew the secret healing there is in flowers and plants: gathering each in its prime and, by means of a rude chemistry, taking out of each its curative essence. Their very names in Gaelic are odorous. The gilly-flower is Half-the-Summer plant. The sweet violet is the Scented Bowl. The bluebell is the Cuckoo's Shoe. And borage was the Courage-giver. Out of it they brewed ' one of the four great cordials.' Whoever drank it drew his sword and thought ten men no match for him. For some of them was claimed a virtue not strictly medicinal, a claim one fervently wishes were true. Thus the smoke of the yellow poppy was said to have the power of expelling evil spirits. Lovage they called the Cajoler's Plant, since its soothing property gave quiet to the mind, while Wild Thyme is an antidote against unpleasing dreams. About others are entwined the tendrils of a sweet tradition, as in the case of Persicaria. A sacred plant, its Gaelic name is the Herb of the Tree. For did it not grow at the foot of the Cross, and did not the drops of the Holy Blood make red its petals! On the other hand, the legend of the Red Modest One—in English the red rattle—has a romantic and even modern flavour about it. An old verse, urging maidens to pluck its delicate pink flowers and to use them as a cosmetic, promises each fair one that, once she does so,

' There is no prince in all the world
Who will not follow thee.'

In his lively diary, which is an account of his journeyings through the English counties between the years 1781 and 1794, Viscount Torrington makes a deft pass at those who preened themselves on having made the Continental Tour. ' If I have seen nothing abroad,' he writes, ' I am a match for most of my countrymen who have seen nothing at home.' Now the weary sea and the mountains that rose up before their eyes like walls kept the islesman and the glensman at home, though, now and then, to be sure, hunger might send them on a foray. The result was that they had time in plenty to watch the pageant of animal life as it passed by from year to year: to note the habits of dogs and horses and sheep and hawks and birds and cattle: to brood on what they saw and so to gain for themselves a picturesque wisdom which they applied to the business of everyday living. This is how it comes about that we Highland people love to place our thoughts in an imaginative setting. You do not, therefore, sleep badly but ' like a sheep in a briar-bush.' A boisterous wind is ' one that would blow the horns off a goat.' A girl does not sing with ravishing sweetness, ' she sends the birds to the trees.' And you will come by an answer to all your whys and wherefores ' when you hap on the cuckoo's nest.' When they speak of necessity they call it ' that which made the roe take to the loch.' And should you get a small gift from a grudging hand you say to yourself, with a smile of pity for the giver, ' that a large egg never yet came from the wren.' Folklore, plant-lore, animal-lore—between them, this charming trinity has given a delicacy of form to Hebridean thought and character that is always fascinating: and a source of never-ending surprise to those who need to be reminded that man does not live by bread alone. And then there is the sea and womankind. His attitude to these are best studied in these pages. But this I would add. The love-songs of all nations and ages have been sung in praise of maidens, their sparkling eyes and rosy lips and marble brows. The test of the worth-whileness of love, however, must always be in its spirit quality: in the bearing of men towards women who are not so young and whose beauty of face God and the years have changed into beauty of soul. The Hebridean passes the test with honour. To the woman who rules his heart he is the courtier ever. As if he glimpsed a captive angel in her or a dream made flesh. So, tho' his sayings about the virago and the slattern are unpleasantly acid, his reverence for true womanhood abides. And nothing reives him of his faith that

> ' As meal is smoother than grain
> So women are finer than men.'

Of all the radiant things that poets have written of their loves none equals the tribute a plain Island farmer paid to his dead wife. ' She had no children,' he said, ' but she might have been the mother of our Lord.'

HARBOURAGE

What I have done in this book is a very simple thing. I have taken the little ships of tradition and custom and legend and history, and I have towed them into port. For years, forlornly and apart, they have floated among my note-books, or drifted past the treacherous shoals of memory. Now they have come to the anchorage of the printed word. My purpose has been to illumine and to strengthen the Faith. The prayers are heart-cries: the occasional poems, banners, for who so cares, to follow after.

CONTENTS

THE HEBRIDEAN WOMAN—IN HER GENTLE HEART A QUEEN

CONTENTS

THE HEBRIDEAN MAN—DREAMER AND DOER BOTH

For every thought of beauty: for every thought that yields the vision of the inner quiet and strength which may be ours through our glad acceptance of it: for every thought which casts the light of Thy purpose upon our pilgrim way we make Thee praise.

THE WILL'S ARMOURY

' Grant us the will to fashion as we feel,
  Grant us the strength to labour as we know,
  Grant us the purpose, ribbed and edged with
     steel,
  To strike the blow.'

It is John Drinkwater's palpitating verse, envisioning a new world of good, created by a new will, re-energised and triumphant. His picture suggests a sleeping force which, awakening, can bestir itself into valiancy and action. The mystic Celt turns aside from such a dream, not as something that cannot be, but rather as something that cannot be apart from God. For ever and for ever a man's will must await the quickening contact of the Divine.

The Cross is on My shoulder
And I am at thy door;
Open then in haste to Me
And be no longer poor.
Better than the yellow gold
Are My love-gifts three,

Truth and peace and power,
Thy will's true armourie.

Thou lovest us to stand upright in Thy sight. With minds eager to greet Thy truth, even though a sword be in its hand. With hearts that joy in pureness. With wills that march like good soldiers along the roads of duty-doing. With such a gentleness in us that another yearns to win its power. In each of us, therefore, deepen our faith in ourselves; in the thing we may be; in what we know of good; in the ends we seek to compass either with hand or brain. Then to our faith, Father, add faith's crowning grace, the knowledge that, with Thee for us, all must be well.

QUESTION AND SWORD

When the shadows fall upon hill and glen: and the bird-music is mute: when the silken dark is a friend: and the river sings to the star, ask thyself, brother, ask thyself, sister, the question thou alone hast power to answer. ' O King and Saviour of men, what is Thy gift to me? and do I use it to Thy pleasing?'

Take me often from the tumult of things into Thy presence. There show me what I am and what Thou hast purposed me to be. Then hide me from Thy tears.

THE VANQUISHMENT OF DOUBT

An autumn twilight. A cottage by the lip of the sea. A young man in haste to greet another morning. An only son, too. His father watched him, and his mother, with hearts pierced by a thousand daggers. Then, suddenly, uprose a fisherman—such a one as sailed with Jesus on Galilee—and said brusquely, ' I am going to pray.' And in his prayer flamed this jewel of faith: ' Give us to see Thy will, and power to walk in its path, and lo! the night is routed and gone.'

When mystery hides Thee from the sight of faith and hope: when pain turns even love to dust: when life is bitter to the taste and our song of joy dies down to silence, then, Father, do for us that which is past our power to do for ourselves. Break through our darkness with Thy light. Show us Thyself in Jesus suffering on a Tree, rising from a grave, reigning from a throne, all with power and love for us unchanging. So shall our fear be gone and our feet set upon a radiant path.

MR NAMELESS SPEAKS A TRUE WORD

'The King is knocking. If thou would'st have thy share of heaven on earth, lift the latch and let in the King.' She was of Eriskay who had this lovely saying. 'Often and often,' she confided, 'did it burn upon my own mother's lips. And she had the hearing of it from her mother's mother who said that all she knew about it was that it had come from the tongue of a nameless one, a servitor of Columba, such a one as crossed the fords for the love of Jesus, and braved the sea-wind for his sake.'

There is a door to which thou hast the key
Sole keeper thou.
There is a latch no hand can lift save
 thine.
Not crownèd brow,
Nor warrior, thinker, poet famed in time,
But only thou.
O heart make haste and bid Him to thy
 hearth ;
Nay, urge Him in.

So shall thy night be gone with all thy
   dearth,
So shalt thou win
Joy such as lovers know when love is told,
Peace that enricheth more than miser's
   gold.

I wait with love's expectancy. Lord Jesus,
trouble not to knock at my door. My door is
always on the latch. Come in, dear guest, and
be my host and tell me all Thy mind.

THE ANSWER

I came to the Cross, the dew still wet upon it, and knelt me down. I cried, ' O my dear Lord wilt Thou not spell me the secret of Thy Passion, of Thy brave out-during of death and pain?' At which He whispered gently, ' Beloved, go and live thy life in the spirit of My dying, in righteousness and love, then truly shalt thou share My victory and taste My peace.'

A WIDOW'S PRAYER

' Thou art our Father, therefore our strength and light. Of which we, who are now at the chair of Thy grace, ask for a portion, so that we may have power to do Thy will, even though it be a cross.'

From a prayer—once her husband's—of a widowed woman who lived in the Island of Mull. This heart-cry broke from her almost every evening when she and her four children knelt together at the feet of God.

WHAT IS HAPPINESS?

Labour and rest, work and ease, the busy hand, and then the stilled thought: this blending of opposites is not merely the great law of being; it is the secret of its joy as well. For, after all, what is happiness but the balance between toil and quiet. The heart pauses in its beat. The pendulum, too, on the completion of its stroke. But the heart must beat; the pendulum move with absolute precision through the arc of distance.

I listened to two men as they lay upon muran, the rough bent-grass of the Isles, and them watching the sun go down. Like a torch red-burning, held by unseen fingers, it flamed and flamed and flamed, encrimsoning the West. The sea beneath us was a mirror broken only by spears of amber light. Far off a speck of gold that was a bird flew toward the sun, like some belated angel winging upward to the Immortal Gate. Mystery and silence! We saw them lift imperious hands as daring us to speak. Yet the younger spoke at last. ' The sea,' he whispered, ' lies under a spell.' But the other would not have it so. ' The sea,' said he,

' is a living creature like you and me. And now it rests.'

Reveal to me the benediction that is mine in having work to do. Help me, each day, to do it with good-will and pride, as being the work Thou meanest me to do. And, sometimes, and most of all when the day is overcast and my courage faints, may I hear Thy voice saying, ' Thou art my belovèd one in whom I am well pleased.'

THE WAYFARER'S SONG

In the South Lands, three generations ago, lived a Joyous Pilgrim of whom his son has left a tender note, telling of how, on a night that blew windily from the hills, his father and he ' knelt together at a turn of the road and prayed.' And then parted, the father to return to his upland farm, the son to trudge the weary miles that lay between him and the spires of a College town. To the curious only a curious tale, but to the spirit-brother of the Christ one that is exquisite. Here is the true heart of Scotland. Here is father-love which gives a son into the keeping of the Best Comrade, then climbs the hill-road back—content. In the seventeenth-century Highlands and the eighteenth one haps upon the same faith. Only, the travelling man prays for himself, and many and many a time this is his cry:

> ' Jesus! my companion be
> On the road I take today
> Through the moor or o'er the sea,
> Thou, for me, be guide and stay.
> Jesus, my sweet lover! place

In the heart of all I greet
Love like Thine that is a grace
To homing men or roving feet.
Up the hill-way, down the glen,
Past the forest edged with broom,
Where the shadows hide the ben,
Where the rivers deepen gloom,
Radiant, I, Thy lovesman go
Free from fear and sain from foe.'

Saviour and Friend, how wonderful art Thou! My companion upon the changeful way. The comforter of its weariness. My guide to the Eternal Town. The welcome at its gate.

THE FOEMEN RIDE BY, BUT QUIET AND LOVE ABIDE

May it not be that we need the literature of a people as a corrective to its history? The Peloponnesian War, for example, raged for a whole generation, a record of savagery unspeakable. True. But within that period Euripides wrote his tragedies and Aristophanes his comedies. And songs were sung. And grape and olive were harvested. And the merry festivals kept. So, too, in the old Highlands we have many a sorry chronicle of feud and slaughter, but side by side with them a vision of the true life of man and of love as the interpreter of that life. Is it not fine to think that, in a time when the winds of hate blew gustily over the west, a man with peace in his heart could pray:

' God, kindle Thou my heart within
A love-flame to my neighbour-kin,
To foe, to friend, to blood-near all,
To brave, to knave, and to the thrall.
O Son of loveliest Mary, Thou,
Before Thee with this prayer I bow:

Kindle Thou in my heart within
A love to Thee and neighbour-kin.'

How wonderful is Thy friendliness toward
me! How deep! How unchanging. Give me a
grace to pass it on.

SOMETHING TO REMEMBER
PRIDEFULLY

Upon a certain fair morning two men sat by a shore laved by an amethyst tide. The one was old. The other had the morning in his eyes. The old man said, ' I love this outspread loveliness, and love to think it everlasting.' ' But how,' said the other, with his eyes upon the grey hair, ' how can you feel that anything is everlasting?' ' Because,' the veteran answered, ' beauty and goodness and love are the soul's elements, and the soul is everlasting.' So the younger hied him on his way, but at a turn of the road looked back, and behold, there was the old man caught in a flood of radiance, his head a crown of silver, a straight resplendent figure like that of a prophet or a king. And, as he looked, his own thought was transfigured. And he whispered to himself, ' Never forget this hour. Never forget this scene. Never forget that you have looked upon an everlasting man.'

A MAN FROM BARRA'S ISLE
SPEAKS WITH GOD

(A kinless one who lived in a moorland house alone)

' Jesus, son of the Virgin-Mother, I rest me on Thy promise that, if only I live for Thee from day to day, I shall yet live with Thee for ever.'

A prayer remembered by a sailor who heard it often on his mother's lips.

' IT IS ALL ONE, THE COMING OR THE GOING'

' It is all one, the coming or the going,
If I have kept the last essential me.'

A modern singer has it that—

' The high soul climbs by the high way.
The low soul gropes by the low.
And, in between, on the misty flats
The rest drift to and fro:
But every man decideth
The way his soul shall go.'

It is just another way of saying that you create your own rank in that most majestical of all the realms, the realm of personality. In it a plain man can be a king, and a king sit upon a throne such as Caesar never knew. If you are simple and kind; if you are pure and just; if, daring to give your will to your conscience, you change your dreams to deeds, then the beautiful thing that happens is that your spirit passes into the spirit of another. You radiate light. And Truth. And Love.

And so march onward down the ages.

Upon a morning in late spring, a man, quiet and toilworn, looked on his dead mother's face, and said, ' My dear one, I thank you for the vision you gave me of the Christ.' At which word it seemed to those who were with him in the room that the mother stirred in her sleep and smiled happily as though she had reward enough.

Seven times a day, as I work upon this hungry farm, I say to Thee, ' Lord, why am I here? What is there here to stir my gifts to growth? What great thing can I do for others— I who am captive to this dreary toil?' And seven times a day Thou answerest, ' I cannot do without thee. Once did my Son live thy life, and by his faithfulness did show My mind, My kindness, and My truth to men. But now He is come to My side, and thou must take His place.'

AN ISLAND PHYSICIAN

The art of healing was thought to run in families: the secret virtue in each herb an heirloom which passed from father to son. As in the case of the Beatons whose skill was a proverb in the mouth of gentle and simple alike. Martin, a sixteenth-century traveller, mentions in his *Western Islands* that he had talk with one of them, a Mr. Neil Beaton, in Skye. About whom he notes that ' he considers his patients' constitution before any medicine is administered unto them.' The curative properties of the various plants were known also to the lave of folk. Thus, Meòir Mhuire (Our Lady's fingers) were a balsam for bruises; Dubhan-ceann-cósach (purnella) was a heal-all; while the wood-sanicle was effectual ' for wounds or whatever other mischief Mars inflicteth on the body of a man.'

O most gentle Physician, Thou hast a balsam for each hurt of ours, be it from ourselves or from another. Thou feelest our spirit's pain in Thine. For Thou and we are kin so close that none can be closer. Therefore it is Thy delight to heal us.

THE THREE WONDERS

' If a man has the fortune to come by a vision of the three wonders: the wonder that God is; the wonder a woman is; the wonder that he is in himself, there is a radiance in his spirit which breaks through his thought and his eyes and his speech.' He was a simple upland farmer who said the words and his face glowed at the truth of them.

Though the dawn breaks cheerless on this Isle today, my spirit walks upon a path of light. For I know my greatness. Thou hast built me a throne within Thy heart. I dwell safely within the circle of Thy care. I cannot for a moment fall out of Thine everlasting arms. I am on my way to Thy glory.

AN ISLANDER'S FAREWELL

You may pour water into any vessel and the thirsty will cry it sweet. Into a king's chalice of gold. Into a peasant's drinking-horn. But beauty you may pour into the cup of the lovely minded only. Seeing that they have understanding of many secret things; as, for example, why the Hebridean's word at parting with lover or wife or friend is perfect of its kind. 'The blessing of God go with you and the blessing of Columba.' 'Strange,' says a man who stands upon the outer rim of knowing. 'Not strange at all,' he smiles who stands within. For to bless another is to pass on your self, to share with him or her something of the spirit of your love and strength. So it comes about that Iona's saint lives on in that warm farewell, his presence at one's side, and his prayer for safeguard.

O Holy Christ, bless me with Thy presence when my days are weary and my friends few. Bless me with Thy presence when my joy is full, lest I forget the Giver in the gift. Bless me with Thy presence when I shall make an end of living. Help me in the darkness to find the ford. And in my going comfort me with Thy promise that where Thou art, there shall Thy servant be.

SOME KINSHIP WITH DIVINITY IN US ALL

From the mouth of a hill-cave two young men watched a tinker man and wife trudge along the road that skirted the still loch which lay at their feet. The travelling ones were making for a stark, wind-battered farm-house such as the Isles show in plenty. A soft July rain was falling, warm as the frothing milk. The young men watched eagerly, perhaps amusedly, for what might happen, since they knew that the family were at the midday devotions. What did take place was this. The gangrel pair, reaching the door and hearing the chanting of a psalm, stood still. The voice of the worshippers rose and fell. They on the threshold did not stir—only they bowed their heads over clasped hands. Then silence. Someone was at the throne, offering the incense of prayer. The moment after they were there too. On their knees in the falling rain, so that to the hidden watchers they seemed no longer beggars whose stock-in-trade was a whine, but angels worshipping the exceeding glory of the Most High.

THE MORNING THAT MAKES
ALL AMENDS

In an isle, a place of note so small that its name finds no mention on the map, a man set out with eagerness upon the last adventure. The dusk made its sacrament in his heart. The sea-music, as though to suit his mood, came to his ears as violins when one is upon the edge of sleep. And now and then he smiled with the tenderness of one who takes a valley road upon a May morning. At last, waking from his visions, he spoke to his wife. ' It darkens,' said he; ' look out, if it be your will, and tell me how it is with the tide.' She looked. ' It flows,' she answered. At this his eyes blazed. ' And when it turns to ebb,' he cried, ' I shall be free. . . . And see the children again! And tell them that your heart to them is just the same!' Her face, framed by the purple of twilight, imaged that eternal sorrow that is a woman bereaved. ' The children?' she queried piteously. ' But are you sure?' For answer he raised his wasted hand and touched her cheek, ' My dearest one,' he whispered, ' that is why I have to go.'

❖

Divinest Three, yet human as we,
Teach us that Here and There are one,
That there's no heaven, unless there be
Meeting and greeting beneath the Tree of Life,
   when faring's done.

❖

As the moorland pool images the sun, so in
our hours of self-giving Thou shinest on us,
and we mirror Thee to men. But of the Other
Land, our heaven to be, we have no picture at
all. Only we know that Thou art there. And
Jesus, the door and the welcome of each faithful
one.

❖

Even though the day be laden and my task
dreary and my strength small, a song keeps
singing in my heart. For I know that I am
Thine. I am part of Thee. Thou art kin to me
and all my times are in Thy hand.

THE SURPRISING DAY

Here is a tale of an Island farmer who went upon an errand of friendship. A day of summer in its prime. A warming sun there was and a west wind—such a wind as stirs the corn to sighing and no more. So, to be sure, he felt himself walking as one in a dream. When he was thankfully home again and had supped, the eager questioning began, and this was the talk that passed between his lady-wife and him.

SHE: Tell me, man of my heart, how things went with you, and what you saw and heard between dawn and the dark feather of the dusk.

HE (*slowly and as one forthcome from a meditation*): Many a wonder.

SHE: Wonders! Pray and what were they?

HE: A sight of jewels there is not the equal of in the land—the Isles strung like emeralds upon the breast of the sea. Still clouds that had the shape, some of castles, some of angels. And a carpet of grasses that was a marvel for softness to the feet.

SHE: Yes, yes. But what else?

HE: Why, I saw a maid and her lover who smiled on me as though in pity; and on the hill, where the Four Winds meet, I had a word with Torquil's widow, Sheena of the Little Glen. ' Is it not the treasure of a noon?' I said heartily. But she only answered, ' Every noon is black to me, since Torquil took leave of living.' I had better luck with Red Finlay, though, for when I came to where the old man was reading the Book in the sun I blessed the day to him too. At which he smiled. ' This,' says he, as if he knew for certain, ' this is a picture of the weather they have in the otherworld every day.'

SHE (*softly*): True is it that your eyes have looked upon many a wonder, man of my heart, beauty and love and sorrow and faith made flesh.

To the Celt each new day is a gift, a flower; above all, a mystery which calls for the companioning of God, if a man would see it well through. Hence the old prayer :

> God be with me
> In this, Thy day,

Every day,
And every way,
With me and for me,
In this, Thy day.

AN ISLAND GIRL PRAYS UPON A JUNE MORNING

This day, I say to myself, is Thy love-gift to me. This dawn, white with the purity of Thy mind, I take it, Lord, from Thy hand, and, for the wonder of it, I give Thee thanks. Make me busy in Thy service throughout its hours, yet not so busy that I cannot sing a happy song. And may the south wind blow its tenderness through my heart so that I bear myself gently towards all. And may the sunshine of it pass into my thoughts so that each shall be a picture of Thy thought, and noble and right.

THE GIVER IS MORE THAN THE GIFT

The saying ascribed to Jesus, the Lord of truth, ' Raise the stone and thou shalt find Me. Cleave the wood and there am I,' suggests that a man may hap upon Divinity everywhere. With courage, of course, must his quest be, and eagerness. And to him who prospers, what a joyful finding ! What an enrichment of my personality to know that every thought in me that is clean and strong is the inbreathing of His mind; that He has planned my capacity; has purposed my love of song or beauty or science; has given me vision to see the kingdom of heaven in a child's smile; has set Eternity within my heart. By all means let us honour the mind, but let us not be so dull or blind as to withhold our worship from its Giver. Is not this the heart of the folk-tale of the beggar who would see the king? Seven times a day did he wish this wish and at last did the wish come true. For a courtier, to whom he had done a service, gained him entrance to the king's levée, or, rather, to a coign of the music-gallery from which he might gaze his fill upon the royal face. But, alas! the carpets were of a blue so rich, the tables of a carving so chaste, the ladies of a beauty so exquisite, and the melody the viols made so tender—sweet as fairy music when the moon is low—that the beggar carle clean forgot all else. Only when the court was over did he mind him that he had not seen the king.

> May I be thrall to beauty
> Through all my days,
> Yet not forget my duty,
> Thy gift to praise.
>
> May the thrush thrill me with
> His passion note,
> Yet, thrilling, mind me 'tis
> An angel's throat.
>
> Give me to trace Thy mind
> In all mind makes,
> In all things fair to find
> Love for our sakes.

Give me a constant trust in the royalty of

my spirit, a trust so high that I dare not live beneath myself. Give me, as well, the vision of what my spirit is, Thy breath and very self in me.

THE END OF THE QUEST

It fell upon an autumn eve that three young Islesmen had talk with one who had served in the wars of the Spirit, and from which he had won back to a victor's peace. Though not unwounded.

The symmetry of the scene was perfect. The scent of hay new-mown; the plashing of oars reaching faintly from the sea-loch below; the sense of separation, which is an island's gift, from tumult and care; the western rim aglow, as though a painter had brushed it over with the three colours of the fairy-pot, rose and amber and gold—each separately and all blendingly laid that spell of peace and beauty on the thought which the musician or poet alone has power to interpret aright.

The talk was of those mysteries that for ever beckon to the adventuring mind. Would the time come, it was asked, when the spirit of man, clothed with capacities now undreamt of, would sail forth and find a new continent of truth, some glorious answer to the riddle that is God and pain and death and immortality? Or does God wait until our eyes can bear the fuller light? Or must we be as wayfarers walking in the twilight of faith with many a weary mile between us and the Eternal Town? Then it was that the host, hitherto silent, had his word. ' There need be no twilight. A man has Christ. Is He not the truth?' he whispered. ' Is He not the light? Is He not the keeper of the treasure we seek so blindly?'

I am bewildered by so many things. I ask myself why the little one is taken from the mother's breast: why the bonds of married love are severed ere even love's noon is come: why the dreams Thou hast sent us reach not the haven of fulfilment. Jesus, Thou Light of men, bring me out of my groping into the radiance of Thy truth. Yet, if Thou withholdest Thy light from me because my eyes cannot bear its brightness, still give me what is needful to make my dark be gone.

ENOUGH AND BEST OF ALL

Three fishermen, three generations, sat in an anchored lobster-boat eating a meal. In such a dream-cove as Gerald Hopkins pictured :

> Where no storms come
> Where the green swell
> Is in the haven dumb.

The August sun made the curve of sand that fringed the bay a flashing scimitar. The tide incoming was full of news; the sea, without, low-murmuring as when a man whispers a tale meant for one ear only. The young man was the first to speak. ' This,' he murmured, ' if it might last for ever, were enough.' He meant—to drink the wine of youth and ever, oh wonder! to find the chalice full: to have his share in laughter and the magic of friendship: the breath of kisses on his cheek and in his body the feel of glory. His father smiled. ' If a man,' said he, ' come to the midst of his years, might be sure of quiet and a full table and some gold in his crock it were enough.' Then the grandfather had his say. ' If a man but knows what is God's will for him and gets him power to do it, it is enough and best of all.' And at his word the silence of seven dawns fell upon their hearts.

O pitiful heart of God, make us meet for the bestowal on us of Thy good Spirit. Since without Him we cannot walk with a high heart: nor come by the secret of the inner quiet: nor give our wills to our conscience.

MY SPIRIT SHALL STILL BE IN ITS YOUTH WHEN THE HILLS ARE DUST

To the north the mountain ranges stood like kings upon their thrones. The sky was an arch of pearl. A cloud city, with towers and battlements complete, went floating by. The mystery of the Infinite was about us. Then the old stalker spoke. ' Is it not fine,' he mused, ' to be abroad upon a day like this? For, look you, the high places win the heart to peace, and here a man gazes on the mirror of his own eternity.'

Heaven and earth are full of Thy glory. Teach me how full. Teach me to see Thee in all things seen and felt and heard: to find in the rose the symbol of Thy creative beauty: in every gentle look the picture of Thy abiding friendliness towards myself.

THE MYSTIC CROWN

As little by little the mind gains a footing within the lordship of truth, its quality of reverence grows. Today a man humbles his thought to wait, to listen, to welcome light from any candle—such a one, that is to say, as has journeyed even a mile or two into its realm magnifical. Your authentic scholar is no scoffer, with the result now that even what seems a cantrip of fancy is no longer elbowed out of reason's court as though it were nothing better than an old wife's tale. Rather are we come to see that mystery is just truth, truth draped and veiled, because our eyes as yet cannot bear her glory. Take the thought of the Mystic Crown. The pure in heart, so the Celtic genius would have it, are sometimes seen to wear an aureole of light and that of a lustre which outshines the sun. In an opal dusk a boat freighted with death made for a rocky islet that gave sepulture to generations of Hebrideans. And one said of him gone to the High Father, ' He was a good man.' An old sailor, plying his oar, agreed. ' He was that, for sure,' fell his word; ' 'tis often these eyes of mine have seen the Mystic Crown upon his brow.' Whereupon the stillness on sky and wave passed into a sacrament. No man looked upon his neighbour's face. The oars beat out an almost unearthly rhythm. It was as though, like Arthur's barge, the fisher's boat were making through quiet seas for a port of heaven.

If I might wear a crown,
It would not be a king's
The trickster, chance, puts on,
And then down flings.

Nor garlanded would be
With Beauty's annulet,
Whose captives praise an hour,
And then forget.

Nor set Fame's diadem
Upon my brow above.
Who would not barter Fame
For a child's love?

Yet, could I win the mystic
Crown of purity,
It were enough—more than
A king's degree.

THE HEBRIDEAN WOMAN—
IN HER GENTLE HEART A QUEEN

AN ANCIENT CUSTOM

A moment after birth, such the tender custom of the Isles, three drops of water were sprinkled on the child. The first drop, in the name of the Father, is the sign of wisdom; the second, in the name of the Son, the sign of peace; while the third, in the Spirit's name, stands for purity. As the weary mother watched the sacred rite, she whispered to the babe upon her breast :

> The blessing of the Holy Three,
> Little love, be dower to thee—
> Wisdom, Peace and Purity.

And many a time spake not again upon the earth.

A HEBRIDEAN MOTHER'S ORISON

Thou seest me, Father, stand before my cottage door, watching my little ones at play. O Thou, to whom to love and to be are one, hear my faith-cry for them who are more Thine than mine. Give each of them what is best for each. I cannot tell what it is. But Thou knowest. I only ask Thou love them and keep them with the loving and keeping Thou didst show to Mary's son and Thine.

THE SECRET OF GENTLENESS

In a great house that gave its back to the meadowlands and its eager face to the sea, there lived, in other days, a most noble lady. The four desires of a woman's world were hers fulfilled—beauty of face: a true man's love: the kisses of children: and plenteousness in warmth and food. But, because she was a king's daughter, He who is wise to know to whom to give a gift added the grace that crowns even a queen. And that was gentleness. So she was the marvel of her kind, a byword for tenderness in the mouth of the Isles.

One nightfall, so the old tale goes, who should come to her door but a wandering saint. To him she gave food and a resting place. On the morrow, ere parting, she asked him whether there was any service she might make him. ' Yes,' said the holy man, ' there is one. Tell me the secret of your exceeding gentleness.' At this the lady mused for long, her eyes downcast; then answered softly as one waking from a lovely dream, ' There is no secret—only—only I am always at His feet, and He is always in my heart.'

Thou knowest how tenderness steals upon me when the sea is still and the wind is lown. Yet, Father, for something more and more abiding do I pray. Even for a constancy of gentleness in myself. Teach me how I may win its secret: through faith in Thee: through faith in love: through Jesus born within my faith.

RENUNCIATION

There was a woman of the glens who had an only son; a right proper lad; tall and very fine to look upon. His eyes had the blue of June hills in them. When he spoke his voice gave out a music like that of a little waterfall heard in a still dusk. A girl watched him smile, and found there was no more heart left in her. And boys vowed that his equal was not to be met with among the peopled Isles. All this was he to his lady-mother and more, the dawn and the noon and the sunset of her dream. For, alas, it came to that. Since he went to the wars and fell. But she died too—not her body, but her courage and her pride and her care for living. And there was no ebb to her grieving. At last in pity God sent her an angel who offered the three gifts of comfort that are wont to salve such as she; the gift that is forgetfulness; the gift of refuge in another's heart; the gift that is His promise of an early meeting in the Upper Garden. But she only said the angel nay. ' Tell the High Father,' she cried, ' that I will heal me of my sorrow when He gives me back my son.' So the angel winged back to the court of light, sore mourning that she, the lady-mother, could not see that to give up a dearest thing to God is to keep it, and that blind are they who close the door upon the offered riches of love.

If sometimes Winter's in my heart
So that I cannot sing
The songs that Beauty made upstart
In me to welcome Spring;

If sometimes in my treasure-room
I weep to find in dust
Dreams that I vow'd should out-brave change,
Like gold secure from rust;

If sometimes Love has proved to be
Less than what poets say;
If she has risen from my hearth
And bowed and gone away;

Yet that brief tenderness of hers
Makes all my gloom take wing;
And if the Winter numbs my dream
Lord! was there not the Spring?

By all I yield teach me to win
Into the truth that Thou
Art moulding some enduring good
Out of what seems loss now.

Thy will be done in me. Thou art my
Father. I am Thy child. Whatever comes to
me, therefore, must be of Thy love's sending.
Father! Thou wilt not hurt Thine own child.

THE LOVE OF GOD IS BROADER THAN THE MEASURE OF MAN'S MIND

The creeds have never put the Islesman's faith in shackles. Nor priest nor presbyter can rob him of the hope that before the last darkness falls the Tireless Herdsman will bring his sheep and lambs into the upper fold, not one miscounted. Of inseeing did any ever say a lovelier thing than the old Highland mother who comforted herself for her son dead in war. ' He was ever a rover,' she whispered as she stirred the peat ash, ' and the blood warm in the veins of him, yet 'twas he who had the mirthful laugh and the giving hand. So, to my thinking, his feet kept God's road. Some journey in sunshine, and fair is their travel; and some, like my lad, push on through the shadows. But it is the same road, and leads at last to an Eternal Town.' The generous man, Columba said, is sure of heaven, for his life is the gospel. And sure too is he who kindles at beauty: he who never sees a man but wishes him well: and he who cries heartily to the wanderer ' Come thou in, brother, and let the night go by.'

Four men met Jesus
At the Door of Fate;
Each man said, ' Jesus,
Is it now too late?'

Then sweet spake Jesus
Like gentlest mother,
' Mind of some love-thought
And tell it, brother.'

The first said humbly,
' I saw a lone glen
That mirrored Thy beauty
For envisioned men.'

' And I,' cried the next,
' Saw my child in tears,
And knew how one wounded
Feels, pierced by spears.'

' Lord Christ,' vowed the third,
' This is wondrous true;
Once I saw boys play
And their angels too.'

Quoth the fourth one thus,
' I know my mother,
And know that God is
Just such another.'

Four men met Jesus
At the Door of Fate;
' Welcome,' said Jesus,
' You are not too late.'

Often I am like a man lost upon a moorland in the mid of night. I listen to the talk of men as to what I must believe, if I would be pleasing to God: if I would see Thy face : if I would know truth. And so my hope falters and my faith swerves. Lord Jesus, set me free from the power of words. Bring me into the place of Thy light. Give me strength to be true to Thee in me. Perfect my faith in our Father. Teach me that what I do each day is the crown and proving of my faith.

THE MOTHER'S BLESSING

In Coll, a gentlewoman used to tell of how she minded of the blessing which her mother gave her the night before she hied her to a city where gold weighs more than love, and folk are too busy to think of the sun or the sea. Her father and the younger children bedded, did not the lovely mother take her daughter to her breast, pouring out all her heart, mingling tears with talk courageous. Long silences and close holding and heart-speech. Then at last the blessing—holy, marvellous, golden words that seemed to her girlish thought to drop from the mouth of God Himself. ' My brothers,' said the old lady with proud assurance, ' got the same blessing as I, and, though we prospered little, yet are we rich in faith and unfearingness.'

Hearken, fair son of my love, to me
Torn with love 'twixt keeping thee
And bidding thy heart
From my heart depart

To win the dream I cannot see.
What'er thy morrow
Of sun or sorrow,
May God go comrade at thy side
His arm thy bield,
His love thy shield,
'Gainst chance's barb or change's tide.

I bless Thee for the secret voice which tells
me I am dear to Thee. I worship Thee because
I know the voice for Thine.

THE WINNING OF SIMPLICITY

The story of the sixteenth, the Reformation century, is printed—a goodly part of it at least—in letters of carmine. As witness the Ribbed Cave of Eigg. There, in 1577, according to the Sibbald MS., MacLeod of Harris 'smoored' the Isle folk, 'men, wives, and bairns, by putting fire to the cave.'

That day, however, threw up a gentlewoman of quality. And of valour not less. All that is known of her is that she was old and solitary. Nothing else. Not even her name. Yet, in what must have been an hour of dule for her, did she say a thing so noble to the slayers of her kindred that it is like to outdure the fame of chiefs, once mighty in the Isles. For, when they stepped into their birlinns crying that, though they had spared her, hunger was but a laggard sword, what did she flame back at them but this word, 'If I get shell-fish and dulse for my portion, the tender water-cress and a drink from the limpid well of Tolain, my need is served and I shall not want.'

Her riposte pulls one's thought by the sleeve. It suggests that the secret of contentment lies in organizing the self in the direction of simplicity. A parable, surely, for our crowded times, a call to prune the growth of desire, an invitation to weigh our wants in the scales of our needs. And the path to such a gain? What can it be but to see to it that our mind keeps to its upland: to love the best with passion, the best in books, in music, in colour, in science, in our neighbour, in ourselves: to abide by the eternities of right and wrong: to bear ourselves Christlikely, that is, with zest and joy in living; and with a radiant trust in Another's care?

Many a time I wish I were other than I am. I weary of the solemn tide: of the little fields: of this brooding isle. I long to be rid of the weight of duty and to have my part in ampler life. O Thou, who art wisdom and pity both, set me free from the lordship of desire. Help me to find my happiness in my acceptance of what is Thy purpose for me: in friendly eyes: in work well done: in quietness born of trust, and, most of all, in the awareness of Thy presence in my spirit.

THE UNCHANGING IS ALL ABOUT US

Said a Hebridean lady, ' 'Tis ill to sit in a room overmuch. Sometimes, when in my little house, I stare at the red of the peat, there will visit me many a troubling thought. Of the long ago. Of the might-have-been. But when they over-vex, these weary guests, I open my door and stare at the sun and the sea.'

Thou hast destined us for change, us and all things Thy hands have made. Yet we fear not. Nay, rather, we are jubilant. Hast Thou not loved us before the world began? What can change bring us but some better thing?

THE MARRIAGE BLESSING

' I am come for the Christ blessing.' She who spoke the eager words was young; lithe as a willow in the wind ; exceeding fair to look upon; with such a splendour of womanhood upon her that she cast a glory on the little room. She to whom the words were spoken was of Mull; hers a disciplined face lit up by two sea-blue eyes of a glow and purity indescribable. A noble creature who had tasted the bitterest bitter, yet could share in another's joy. One who felt the pain a nestling feels fallen from its nest, and held that a child's glee cannot be set to music. In short one of the holy women of the Isles—of the lineage of Enoch, the companion of God. To such a one the maidens, before marriage, were used to come for blessing. Without might be the sea-music, or the sigh of the west wind caressing the wild violet, but within was a stillness deeper and sweeter than a forest's in mid of winter. A lovely picture. Youth and beauty at the knee of age and pity. No wonder that the benediction fell upon the young girl's ears like a word from heaven: that a new realm of purity gleamed bright before her eyes, and that the angels were so near that she might put forth a hand and touch a wing. For was it not a peerless moment. In it she felt herself the mistress of her fate, and might front tomorrow unfearingly.

' Be with me and for me, dear Lord, as I walk upon the road of brightness that runs between earth and Thy glory.'

From the prayer of an old farmer in the Island of Coll.

THE HEART OF THE FATHER IS A MOTHER'S TO INFINITY

' There is a mother's heart in the heart of
God. And 'tis his delight to break the bread
of love and truth for his children.'

—A Hebridean mother.

I do not think that I shall fear Thee when I
see Thee face to face. For I call to mind my
father, he who was the true man and the kind.
And my mother, the pure one, out of whose
heart flowed the waters of healing. And, as I
think of them, my pulses beat with joy and I
cry to Thee, Father, and say: ' Thou art more
and tenderer than they.' Therefore when I am
come into the court of Thy presence I know
that Thou wilt look upon me with my father's
eyes and with my mother's pity and that Thou
wilt draw me to Thy breast.

THE INTERPRETATION OF ILL HAP

The mystic finds truth, like Shelley, at the bottom of the well. The Hebridean plumbs its depth unfearingly. Hence his faith that in the heart of every experience lies a benediction, and that every ill hap opens a door to some larger good. Upon a certain May morning a blind woman sat delighting in the glory of it. At her feet a young girl who stared at dreams that rode mistily by. ' And what,' said the blind one, ' is the likeness of the sea today?' The girl answered, ' Like a maiden vestured in pale-blue silk and it rippling softly in the wind.' ' Ah! the blessed wind,' said the other, ' clover and music in it the live-long day. The very breath of the dear God and a purpose in every gust of it. But then,' the brave voice went on, ' there is a purpose in all things and whoso finds it wins strength to bear. I am blind but well content and my contentment is my use to God.'

Show me Thy purpose in my cross, so that, like Jesus, I may win strength to bear it.

ONE LOVELINESS IS OURS FOR EVER

One jewelled page, at least, in the book of memory—however brown and wan the others, is there not always one? portrait of one exquisite face that looks out from between the frames of yesterday with a glance so warm and loving that the heart-beat quickens? A woman's? Or the only man a woman would have trudged with to the world's end? Faces serene and strong; infinitely patient; unchangeably quiet!

' I knew a wonder woman,' a man of the Long Island said once, ' who was perfect in herself. Her eyes were pools of quiet. And the sea-sweetness rang in her voice, and when she smiled it was June.'

Once, my Father, I thought that the faces of my dear ones were the fairest earth or Heaven could show. Now I see that every face is fair that is the flesh of Thy thought. And often there will come to me a longing to see the face of Jesus, since, till then, I

shall not know what love and perfect purity
are like.

FAITH VEILS A POWER
EXPERIENCE TURNS TO GAIN

As well as shores the Isles have glens; far from the cry of the sea; temples of stillness where the plash of the burn is the only music, the winds the only incense, the stars the only candles.

In one such dwelled a small farmer and his wife. An ailing one she, a blown flower, so sick of body that her daughter forsook the calling that she loved, and came to her.

A sun-haired queen she was, a noble creature, and lithe as any soldier. Her mind, too, was like her face, fair to look upon, so that it was a joy to listen to the eager speech of her. Her favourite image about the business of living was that it is a campaign. ' Every one,' she used to say, ' fights with something. My brother fights with the sea, my mother with her pain, my father with his farm, and I with myself and'—remembering all that she had cast behind her and that lay before her—' and to believe that God is just.'

As the rain hides the stars, as the autumn mist hides the hills, as the clouds veil the blue of the sky, so the dark happenings of my lot hide the shining of Thy face from me. Yet, if I may hold Thy hand in the darkness, it is enough. Since I know that, though I may stumble in my going, Thou dost not fall.

LOVE LOVES TO PRAY

South Uist, the Catholic Isle, is fortress still and shelter to many a fair heritage of thought; and to a faith majestical.

A little old dame, driven from it by the goad of want, to another island a ferry-throw away, deemed her fate an exile's. ' I and my dear flesh in Canada,' was her constant plaint, ' are far from home, earth's heaven, the machair lands of Uist.' Yet memory was a sun that shone upon the treasure of her youth, and when she spoke of her mother it was ever through a lustre of tears. ' The eyes of the Blessed Virgin,' she would say, ' were her eyes, blue as the sea but kinder, and her voice rich and low as a harp heard in dreams. A minding comes to me of how each night, when she thought me sleeping, she would croon the sleep-prayer to be made to God for little ones. And of how she would ask our Father to send down the Protecting Three to be my guard, the Watchful Angel, the Angel of Peace, and the Angel of Health.'

71

O Thou who art high,
Send down from the sky
The Angels Three,
That while I sleep,
My babe they keep
From harm and fear.
So shall I feel
That Thou art near
When they are nigh,
And myself sleep
Without a care,
Without a sigh.

Once, with dreams before our eyes, we prayed for our children, prayed that their voyaging might be that of ships that sail with favouring winds over a summer sea. We asked that life for them might be an easeful and radiant thing. Now, with a clearer vision in us, we ask that Thy spirit may dwell in theirs, making their desires pure, and kindness the law of their thought. Once we asked that no grievous thing might touch them. Now we ask that whatever discipline the years may bring them shall perfect their trust in Thee.

THE HAPPY PRINCESS

There is a happy Princess in old Celtic legend who, every year, comes tripping over the summer hills and sings with such enchantment that the fisher ceases from sea-toil; women from the spinning-wheel; the little ones from play, nay even the merle from his piping. ' I love,' she sings, ' and I am loved, and so know joy for friend.'

I am serene because I know Thou lovest me. Because Thou lovest me, naught can move me from my peace. Because Thou lovest me, I am as one to whom all good has come.

A GRANDMOTHER'S BENEDICTION

The glory of a woman, so the copy-books have it, shows in the quality of her love, its deathlessness, its self-giving, its refusal to be slain. But in that valour of mind, which is hers, abides a splendour not less. And a magical swiftness too, her judgment an arrow piercing to the heart of truth. As though God has gifted her with a secret power of knowing! As though a vision of reality kept burning before the eyes of her spirit.

A dame, aged and bent, the musics of wind and sea blending in her voice, gathered a tiny bundle that was her grandchild to her withered breast. And blessed him thus : ' I bless thee, darling one, in the name of the Holy Three, the Father, the Son, and the Sacred Spirit. Thine may it be to drink deeply from God's cup of joy. May the sun be bright upon whatever road thou farest. May the night bring thee quiet. And when thou art come to the Father's palace may His door be open and the welcome warm!'

Only an island-woman was she who spoke these words, yet, once spoken, all there knew

that this was the loveliest wish to wish a child,
and that she had gathered into her heart-prayer
all the ancient wisdoms of saint and scholar
and seer.

Wilt Thou not yield me vision,
Lord of Grace,
Of that vast realm
Of unhorizoned space
Which is Thy heart
That heart-room makes for all?

A MAN WITH EIGHTY SUMMERS BEHIND HIM WATCHES THE ISLAND CHILDREN PASS ALONG THE SHORE-ROAD ON THEIR WAY FROM SCHOOL

I send my heart to Thee in thanks for these little ones: for the strange uprising of happiness that comes to me as my eye follows them. Sweet is the music of their wind-borne laughter, yea, sweeter than all musics. I listen to them, and am one with the mavis and the dawn and the flower. And then I wonder what Thy thought is of them—Thy children. Yet I need not wonder. For I look upward and lo! Thou art leaning out over the window of Heaven, and Thou art smiling.

THE KINGDOM OF LIGHT

A woman of Jura had the story, and sweet upon her lips was the telling of it—the story of how a Princely One gained for himself the kingdom of light.

First did he strive with a giant whose name was Fear, and him slew. And then with Doubt, his kinsman. That was a long and dreadful field, but ' Mark you,' said she, ' my love put death on him as well.' And then, with mirth in his eyes did he set out for his fair estate, there to rest and heal him of his wounds. But, like some before him, the Princely One found that wishing and having are two towns with many a weary league between. For, as he journeyed on, still another foeman barred the way, one who was a lion for fierceness and the might of seven in his sword-arm. His awful name was Self. With him the Prince fought a thousand battles, but in the end was victor. So by and by he came to his realm which was of such a loveliness that he clean forgot his travail. ' It was worth it all,' he cried, ' and for all that is past a high requital.'

Of soft musics is there aught to vie with the

dulcet note of the canach flower blowing in the south wind? To our straining ears, when the tale was done, the Jura woman's whisper seemed every whit as tender. ' My dear ones,' she murmured, ' there is a prince in every man and, at hand for the taking, a kingdom of light.'

All that I am Thou hast made me. All that I have Thou hast given. And given and made that I may image Thee. May I be equal, therefore, to Thy hope of me. If I am weak I ask that Thou send me only what I can bear. If I am strong may I shrink from no testing that shall yield increase of strength or win security for my spirit.

THE PEARL OF PRICE

There was a woman in a certain isle who was a wonder to many; lovely of face, gracious of bearing, so soft of voice and so splendent of mind that she might have mated with a king. Yet her husband was a shy man; given to silence and the companionship of the hills. Only once did she raise the veil. And that was when she said, ' I sold my dreams for love, and found love better than all my dreams.'

Break upon our blindness with Thy light. Show us, whatever we deem loss, that love is final gain.

SUNS EVER AT THEIR NOON

A Gaelic saying, chiselled out of the rock of experience and perfect in its tenderness, is, ' An dà mhaireann, gaol na máthar agus grádh Dhè'—' The Immortal Twain, the mother's love and the love of God.'

When the mountains skip across the
    plain,
And dance upon the sea,
Then will thy mother's heart be dead,
Thy mother's love to thee.
When trees shall whisper to the stars,
' Our loneliness is wrong;
Come, let us break these age-fast bars
And chant our freedom's song,'
Then will thy mother's love be slain
By spears than death more strong.

.   .   .   .   .

O little son, I bend me down,
And lift thee to my cradling breast,

And murmur, ' Why this madness sing,
Since Love outlasteth everything.'

THE MOTHERHOOD OF GOD

I have a secret joy in Thee, my God. For, if Thou art my Father, Thou art my Mother too. And of Thy tenderness and healing and patience there is no end at all.

THE HEBRIDEAN HEIRSHIP—
TALES HALF AS OLD AS THE SEA

CAOINEAG

Caoineag, the Fairy Weeper passes through
the glens and corries of Highland legend with
a step so shy and with a mien so tender that
one almost forgets that she is an ambassadress
of woe. Not that she wished to be but, black
the day ! she had to be since she, who was
cursed with the two seeings, ever looked at
tomorrow within the womb of today. Oft and
oft on the eve of battle did she see battle
joined ; and men fall ; and stir not. A fairy's
body was hers, but a woman's pity : yet might
she not show it : nor had she any charm against
the thrust of fate. The night before Culloden
three women met at the Well of Sorrow in
Aberarder of Strathnairn to draw water ; also,
doubtless, to speak those words, warm and soft
and secret, that woman tells to woman only.
But, alas ! for the doleful tryst. For as they
talked of their sons who were Charlie's men,
what reached them, borne upon the breast of
the April wind, but the weeping of a woman.
Slow and low it was. Terrible as Rachel's who
would not be comforted. Rising and falling
like a piper's coronach and him marching

through a glen forlorn. ' It is the Fairy Weeper,'
they cried in horror, and fled. And so, the
story goes, it was. Their heart-loves came not
back again.

I saw the Fairy weeping
In a hazel dell
Where Quiet her court was keeping,
And knew that ill betiding
Did her tears foretell.
—Death to his feast fast riding !
I heard the wind, her wooer,
Chide ' But why this silver rain,'
Can thy dirge one wound recover,
Or give breath to Love once slain?'
Then I heard the weeper answer,
' Ah, thy wit doth lack the skill
For to understand mine ill,
Since my weird it is to bear
Dule that none with me may share,
Since in these enmirrored tears
I behold the thrusting spears.
Since I cannot cloak tomorrow
From mine eyes, which fain would borrow
Blindness that I might not see
Death exult in victory.'

Then, as tho' she might not stay,
Leaping burn and breasting ben,
Went the fairy on her way
Softly weeping,
As one weeps
Who, now and then,
Minds of Youth and
Beauty sleeping
In a far glen
In a swound that brooks no waking
In a dark that knows no breaking.

Today, frankly, a disciple's faith is more discerning. We have climbed a hill from which the view we get over Truth's realm is both clearer and fairer. Nothing of hate, as we can now see, nothing of sternness lives within our Father's heart toward any of His children. Only holiness. Only love. So, to a perfect trust, the haps and mishaps of our wayfaring are but steps upon a road that lead us to the breast of God. Voices that cry to us to cast our heart upon the Heart Divine: that whisper to our amazements that every loss is but gain in the making : and that final separation of spirit from spirit, and of all spirits from the

Source of Spirit, is something that can never be.

Ennoble our thought with Thy thought of us, the thought of the great thing we may be. Thou hast given into our keeping the trust of life. Make us the servants of its glory, duty, and love.

THE THREE COMRADESHIPS

The gangrel folk were long familiar in the Isles. Kindly they bore themselves ; a courteous tribe, and much given to soft speaking since they had learned the truth of the old Gaelic proverb that ' politeness goes far in a day.' The children of the wild, the wandering heritage of the Celt ran deep in their blood. The open road was their sanctuary, and every season a benediction. Above all things they rejoiced to own themselves. What if the silver rain made them sodden, or the sun blistered, or the wind browned, were they not free !

Said the thriving man to the tinker's wife,
' Spell me the secret of your happy life.

' I could not bide it, I was never made
To couch in bracken with the birch for
    shade.

' And hills I love not, their ironic smile

Seems scornful of the things I hold worth
   while.

' Nor am I ravished of the woodland note
That breaks in tumult from the merle's apt
   throat.

' Yet you love them all. But why? What's
   the art,
That turns rose-petal into quiet of heart?'

' Ah, easy to answer,' she softly said,
' I'm richer than you—that's your riddle
   read.

' Have you heard fir-music? Or the
   whisp'ring tales
That the tide brings in when the white
   moon pales?

' Or glimpsed the slim grace of the tall
   June grass
Bowing demurely to the winds that pass?

' Or strayed through a glen where wild
   violet grew
And thought, "Well, Heaven will be
   nothing new?"

' So I envy none—if I'm poor, I'm free
To the feast love spreads for the like o'
   me.'

Yet while truth is here, while this fair earth of ours pays quittance to all who love her with vision, comradeship with her is not the most gainful a man may come by. For in the companionship of personality, mind with mind, and love with love, breathes a warmth and nearness she cannot offer. And in the soul's commerce with God a fellowship that is best of all.

Persuade me, Thou who lovest me best, that I gain all things when I believe in Thee with a perfect believing. Since such a mind in me releases Thy power for my needs today; makes me safe against the unknown tomorrow, and sure that the best is yet to be.

DAY'S END

Beside the unresting sea and in the far glens stood the small houses of the Gael, bare of comfort as the hills in winter ; a bield from the wind; a covert from the tempest ; and sometimes not even that. Yet these rude dwellings housed a passionate faith. When Night, the herdsman who brings all living things to his fold, had turned the key on care, when talk was done and the world grown still, the family standing in the dim light of the cruisie chanted the praises of their lover, the Christ.

> There is no bird on the wing;
> There is no star in the skies;
> There is nothing beneath the sun
> But forth Thy goodness cries;
> Jesus, Jesus, Jesus,
> Thou art our soul's high prize.

As the tide re-flows to the shore, as Spring returns to the tree, as feet that wander far come back to the old home, so our faith returns to the promise of Jesus, 'If ye shall ask anything in My name I will do it.' Therefore we cry, 'Lord, give us our heart's desire. In how we think and in how we love give us the power to be pure.'

THE TRYST

In his *Ancient Irish Poetry* Kuno Meyer notes that the bells which called the brothers prayerwards, in the early Celtic monasteries, were tongueless. They were struck, not rung; and he quotes an exquisite verse in which a monk, hurrying to nocturne, expresses the famine of his spirit for the bread of God. It is here freely translated.

Sweet little bell,
Thy wind-borne call
Importunate
Bids me arise
Lest I be late
And so should miss
The Bridegroom's kiss,
Love's last surprise.
Did ever bell
Make chime like thine,
Or urgent cry,
' Thy Lord is near,
Lest He pass by
Come here, come here?'

For the Celt—Irish or Scottish—it is a truly magical bell. It rings, and in a moment he is walking in a world where the Faith brings high adventure to the soul: where a man forsakes desire to find his God and where the finding is better than his dream: where spirits cry in the sea-wind, and angels whisper the secrets of Heaven, and the brother of Christ hastes to the rude shrine with feet more eager than a lover's to a tryst. Much has been said against the later ideals of monastic life, and much of truth. To float a straw upon the stream of custom, or to close the ears to the imperious bugles of duty—neither of these attitudes can rank with the faith and courage that dares to grapple with things as they are, and that seeks, in the Divine companionship, to mould them into things as they should be. Yet who can be a judge of his neighbour's duty? That aside, the ruined cells of the Hebrides, are they not muted voices that whisper, that although the Good Father meets the ever-changing needs of His children's spirit through new and ever-changing forms of service and of faith, none the less and well did these Knights of the Cross play their part? ' They loved Christ much and themselves little or not at all,' an Island woman said as she knelt by a tumbled mound. Just was her word and lovely—a window through which a wise man gazes at the Saints.

Giver of the increasing good, take my thanks for all that has made me what I am; for all my yesterdays; their discipline; their pleasant songs; my unanswered prayers, nay even for those whelming hours in which I have seen how frail I am without Thee. And, when tomorrow comes with a new duty or with a new truth, may the door of my mind be open, and I at the door to bid them welcome.

SANCTUARY

Whether or not the caim—the circle which the devout Columban drew round him in the hour of evil's onset—is a heritage from Druid rite, has been much in dispute. The Island faith was that the soul who traced it was safe, entering in a moment into that

> ' City not built by any hand,
>   And unapproachable by sea or shore,
> And unassailable by any band
>   Of storming soldiery for evermore.'

Three spoilers, it was said, prowled at the outer gate of the heart; the first, ready to reive it of its cleanness; the second, of its power to love; the third, of its peace. But, as an ancient dame of Barra put it, ' in such a peril, draw the caim about thee, and thou art in a tower.'

Alas there is a fourth robber the circle has no power to bespell. His name is Death. He steps over it boldly. No incantation halts him. Yet whoso dares to look him in the face finds it an angel's.

In the Name of the Three,
In the name of their might
I will draw the ring
That doth instant bring
Safety from foes' affright.
In the Name of the Three
I shall rout all my fears,
I shall stand all unscathed
From the cast of their spears :
Thus shall I know no overthrow.

I sit upon the shore, Father, watching the face of the waters and the sun-bright clouds; and the mystery of being stills my heart to awe. Then I think of Thee, and then, though mystery lingers, my fear of it is gone. I say to myself that, beyond the empires of space and light, reaches Thy power to be my friend. Wherever I go, whether through a strange land or upon the dark sea-breast, Thou art with me. Therefore I may be quiet of mind.

THE ART OF JOY

The Celt is a pastoral. Hills and herds are his kingdom. Has he not wandered over continents three times a thousand years finding hope in every dawn, and in the sun-going a fresh baptism of wonder? Yet always, through all that long wayfaring, his faith, which is his philosophy, has not changed. And that is, that what one is, is more than what one has; that work and struggle are things by which, not for which, a true man lives; that happiness is simply fortune found. Perhaps for this very reason the Celt is perishing from the earth where the machine has made its maker a thrall. But whether or not, there can be small doubt but that a wiser race than ours will go to his school and re-learn his secret, the art of joy. The Hebridean, for whom happiness is breath, finds it along every mile of the road, and every mile more wonderful than the last. ' It is you who are the foolish one,' rasped a sectarian to a Harris woman and her singing on a June morning as she walked through the machair land with meadow-sweet at her breast, ' you, a mother of children, decked in your silly flowers and carolling an old love song as though it were the praise of God.' To which she murmured in pity, ' But it is the praise of God, and as for my flowers, have I not heard them cry a thousand times how proud they be of their beauty?' The obdurate one did but listen and then go sourly on his way. Light cannot flood a room which has no windows.

'   I am fair'—thus the Island lass
   To the dame at the fire.
' My face a flower, men say.
But I am more than my face.
I have dreams. I share with my race
A passion to find me the way.
Dreams are fleshed into deeds and stay.'
But the dame said, ' Nay,
Dear, exult in your face;
In the tender grace
You see in your glass.
Ere the flower shall pass,
Take joy in its perfect day.'

As the hand is made for holding and the eye for seeing, Thou hast fashioned me for joy. Share with me the vision that shall find it everywhere : in the wild violet's beauty; in the lark's melody ; in the face of a steadfast man; in a child's smile ; in a mother's love ; in the purity of Jesus.

THE GUARDIAN OF CHILDHOOD

Conal—the very whisper of his name made the Hebridean mother warm at the heart, warmer than a man is with meat or cordial. For is he not the Keeper of Children—the little foolish ones who run into peril with as much heeding as the wind blows over the sea! Strong in love for them is Conal, the unseen playmate, the escort who is so close to them that he comes between them and their shadows. Once, so a hearth-tale has it, a small lass sent on an errand was lost in the black of night, such a night of cloud and rain and thunderings as the Isles had never seen. They who sought her came back with empty hearts. But at midnight the door opened gustily and the little maid walked in. And not a rain-drop on her cheek. Nor even a hint of disarray among the golden curls. And this was the talk between her and her mother:

THE MOTHER : Tell us, fair love, how you won through the storm?
THE CHILD : A kind tall man kept at my side.
THE MOTHER : But the mist!

THE CHILD : He blew it away with one mighty breath.

THE MOTHER : And the cloud!

THE CHILD : He lit a candle that made night like day.

THE MOTHER : But the rain?

THE CHILD : He put his hand above me. I heard it pattering, but that was all.

THE MOTHER : And the dark, swift river, how did you compass that?

THE CHILD : Oh that was easy, Mother. The kind one waved a wand and the river divided and we crossed without any trouble.

So when her telling was done they knew that it was Conal she spoke of. And they rose and sang a hymn of praise to the High Father for his gift to children of the Guardian Friend.

A bird flies over the sea, and I, wondering, ask whither. Thou answerest, ' I am its guide. I am the strength of its tireless wing. I choose its secret path. I bring it to its rest.' Make me to be still, Lord, with the happy thought that Thou art doing the like for me. Be Thou my refuge and my song. Let me be as one who knows Thou knowest the way I should go: as one who is sure that the end of the journey is Thy breast.

THE SUN IS GAY ON EASTER MORN

A hundred years ago there were Isles folk who believed that in honour of the Risen One, the sun danced every Easter morning over the floor of the sky. With mad delight—with laughter. As who would not to the music of violins which the archangels play in laud of Him who gave Death his wound. What a madcap fancy! Possibly. But what a beautiful one as well! Is there not breadth and vision, even a reach of majesty in the faith that sun and wind, mosses and flower and sea share in the Resurrection joy of men, and that men should think it not strange at all.

I climb a secret hill
Each Easter morn;
Not for to breathe my fill
Of wonder born
Anew on such a day;
But, move to hear
A trump immortal sound
Within mine ear,

A noise of viols
And a beat of drums,
Bugles that cry,
' He did not die
For aye;
Behold He comes,
Victor from Death's
Red fray.'

I find Thee throned in my heart, my Lord Jesus. It is enough. I know that Thou art throned in Heaven. My heart and Heaven are one.

THE CHARM-FLOWER

The Dawn is a lovely miracle; the changeful sea a picture of the inconstancy of fortune; Night is the sister of Death. That the Hebridean thought in this wise in the bygone time is not surprising, a mystic living in a world that he could not explain to himself. A ' world, therefore, he partly feared and from whose elfin power he wished to be safe. Hence men, but most of all women, longed for safety and mind-peace, as one in a coracle, storm-driven, longs for the quiet of harbourage. Hence, also, did the Islesfolk nurture faith on charms, on sacred wells, on runes spoken seven times at mid of day, on crosses, names of saints and guardian flowers. The dust of bog-violet in a golden amulet had a potency against which the wiles of evil were vain. Whoso wore such was secure: from all despite: from the sorrow of love ungiven: from a foeman's stroke: from the gnaw of hunger: or from drowning, the doom of the sea.

Because I smile
When clouds bedim the sun,
Because I'm still
Of soul when tidings run
That should disquiet,
'Tis said by some
That I must wear
Armour of angels,
Or, at least, must bear
A fairy shield bespelled,
To turn aside the lunge of spear
Which is another's hate;
The lie that soon or late
Thrusts its fierce barb into
My spirit's side.
Friend, think not so,
For all I wear
Is the bright flower of faith
Upon my heart;
Faith that exultant cries,
' Fear not this hour,
God takes thy part.'

I say to myself each night, ' The dawn will
come and all this dark be gone.' I watch the
tide's far ebb and whisper, ' It will flow.' In the

mid of Winter I cry to my heart, ' soon the green banners of the Spring will blow through the land.' Yet surer still I am that Thou art my friend. For Thou hast wrought a miracle in my thought. Thou hast changed faith to knowledge, and hope to sight.

THE SEA-FARER'S CHANT

Be Thou Thyself the guiding star above me,
Lighthouse be Thou for every reef and shoal,
Pilot my barque upon the crest of sea-wave
To where the waters make no moan or roll.
O the restful haven of the wandering soul!

This, is it not a matchless prayer for fishers of every race and age? The Hebridean, with but a plank between him and the sea-bed, murmured it a thousand times. As he did so, his vision bore him to some still port far from the breaking seas, some secret haven where the green swell is dumb, and children play upon the pearl-white sand.

Give us the mind of Jesus, something of His brave heart, as we sail over the waters of experience. And days of sunshine. And favouring winds. And stars to be our guide when the sun is set. Yet this is but half our asking. Lord of pity, when trouble rises, as a storm, turning our trust to fear, bring us into the quiet place of Thy presence and be our haven.

THE BATTLE THAT MUST BE

The last fight is won long before it is ever fought, by glensman and island man. The armour of faith girded on, how serenely these simple men and women bear themselves against the hosts of doubt and fear! Since well they know that Captain Great-heart leads the foreguard. So they go singing through the valley :

When Thou shalt close this mouth of mine,
Mine heart lose power to sob,
When my breath shall cease to rattle,
When my pain shall cease to throb,
Then relieve me, and receive me,
And conduct my soul to God.

When Thou whisperest to me, as Thou wilt some day, that Thou hast need of my company, be Thou the strength and quiet of my spirit.

MAGIC AND TRUTH MUST FOEMEN BE

The Hebridean of the olden time kept a watchful eye upon the bird-world, and the delightful bird proverbs that have come down to us show how tender and understanding such a watching can be.

The crow, for example, and the hoodie were the objects of his misliking—did they not wear black, the livery of sorrow! the sea-gull, symbol of grace and freedom, he loved ; while, in his view, the stone-chat, the wren and the cuckoo were almost sacred. But this because these three are fairy birds. Knowing nothing of the law and instinct of migration, he came to imagine that, during the songless months, they lodged within the fairy bowers. An easy step, therefore, to believe that they had borrowed elfin powers of good or ill. And the believing went from lip to lip and, so, the heredity of fear passed on.

The marrow of the Christ's news, however, is that you may overcome any heritage ; that resources, divine and infinite, are yours for the asking and that, once you don the unindentable cuirass of faith, there is no battle against self or evil or spectre which you may not win. It was a Covenanting Statesman who would have us mind ' that Love, and Power in the service of Love, sit at the helm of the Universe.'

I lift my eyes upward to the abiding hills. I lose myself in wonder as I watch the sky. I bow before the wisdom of Thy law which gives the star its course and the bird its nest. Yet I am greater far than all my eye can see. For Thou hast made me greater. I am the birth of Thy mind, and Thy heart is restless till my heart is Thine.

' 'TWAS BUT A STEP FOR THEIR VICTORIOUS FEET'

' 'Twas but a step for their victorious feet
From the day's walk into the golden street.'

The quest for certainty about the life unending sets the mind upon a march which seems to know no end at all. Yet Faith, which brings the higher knowledge to birth, lays the treasure at our feet. And so it comes about that in every burgeoning spring, in every autumn leaf, in every summer shower, the faith-gifted find in the law of growth and perishing nothing to alarm—nothing except a Divine process of change which issues not in death but in life abundant. The Celt is of this company. He deems himself an immortal; his being the mystic eye which pierces the veil between here and there, and knows them for the inseparable one. And a throne behind the veil. And a king. Which is the reason why every legend offering aid to a man's believing gets welcome at his spirit's door. As that one, for example, of the skylark's song. In Gaelic it goes by the name of Mary's bird, and is,

therefore, sacred. No Highland boy will rob
her nest. For he who reives a single egg is
cursed with as many curses as there are spots
upon the lark's tongue, and every curse
shortens the robber's life by a day. Mary's bird
is she, so the old tale runs, because she trilled
above the Cross, and Mary, listening, knew
her Son immortal. Here is a verse of the lark's
song :

> Nor wound nor spear can ever slay
> My deathless King.
> Since every wound's an open door
> Thy spirit's wing
> Scarce brushes in its upward soar
> To where God waits
> To greet the Son,
> The red field won—
> Well won and more.

Reveal me to myself. Show me the three-
foldness of myself. That I am a body. That I
am myself and apart from Thee. That I am
eternally part of Thee. Then grant me, Lord,
the glory of Jesus. Make me one with Thee.

A SEA-BENISON

The sea breaks upon the mind, as upon the shore, with wave upon wave of mystery. The light of the sun, as with so many of our human ills, does not make its dark secret the less. At dawn, we sense through it infinity. At dusk, the echo of the world's sorrow. At mid of night, the star-candles all blown out, 'tis a brave wayfarer who can hasten by a rocky shore and not be chilled in spirit. The Celt, like the Jew, has ever feared the sea, yet yielded to the sea-magic. And he has adventured as gallantly as most across its unquiet breast, though, to be sure, the end of his voyaging has meant more to him than the joy of it. The mind-picture of anchorage in some little port has drawn him on throughout the centuries as a maiden's face draws a lover. And when the port was won and the tossing waves behind, then did the Hebridean sailor speak to God this lovely prayer :

Father of Powers, by whose sure guiding
We have cleft the deep,
Now underneath Thy brooding wings of love
Grant us the boon of sleep.

Jesus, Lord of the calm and of the storm, whatever seas I sail upon, be Thou my helm, my compass, and my port.

LOYALTY IS STILL THE SAME

The creed of honour-keeping runs through the Highland spirit like red through the tartan. It is the breath of our thought. It is the secret of our courage. It is the glory of our race. Did we not lay the Roman eagles in the dust? And have we not given many a crimson proof, from Flodden to Drumossie, that

> Loyalty is still the same
> Whether we lose or win the game.

In his *Carmina Gadelica* Dr. Carmichael quotes the tradition that the young hunter was bidden to bear himself honourably towards even the creatures of the wind. ' He was not to take life wantonly. He was not to kill a bird sitting, nor a beast lying down . . . the mother of a brood, or the mother of a suckling.'

> Son of my flesh,
> Ere forth thy foot
> Shall set to climb
> The secret hill,
> Or thou shalt go

To hunt the roe,
Or get thee for
Thy seeking fill,
The law of fairness do thou write,
For sun to gild, upon thy heart.
For lust to kill shalt thou not smite,
Nor mother love pierce with thy dart,
Rather bear hunger, than thy faith
Broken should bring thy soul to skaith.

I worship Thee in me. I glow to think that all of nobleness Thou hast mated to my spirit is of Thee, all of self-giving. Give me power, therefore, to do lovely things always. Fashion me so that I must walk with Thee upon the height.

THE SMOORING OF THE PEAT-FIRE

Down the dim centuries the Isles-folk have burned the scented peat. It is a vestal fire, never allowed to die out, since in many of these treeless islands wood is as scarce as gold. They smoor it therefore. In other days, with three peats and always in the name of the Holy Trinity, and always, too, to the chanting of a simple rune :

>The Sacred Three
>My fortress be
>Encircling me.
>Come and be round
>My hearth, my home.

>Fend Thou my kin
>And every sleeping thing within
>From scathe, from sin.
>Thy care our peace
>Through mid of night
>To light's release.

The night falls upon the Isles. As I sit before this dying peat-fire I watch the faces of those dear ones who once lived with me in this house. Of them some now walk in the Upper Garden; others dwell in the far lands. If I moan a little, sigh a little, and say to myself—how brief a guest is joy!—Thou wilt forgive. Then I remember that whether in the body or out of the body, my kin and I are members of Thy family, that one great family which is both in heaven and on earth. Then all my dark is gone.

BLESSING THE MEAL

The passing of the quern, the grinding stones for meal, is mourned by some. Only in Arabia does it survive, and that because the children of the Prophet are set upon an endless quest for victual. They must march or die, as Charles Doughty tells us in his *Arabia Deserta*. They are, therefore, for ever on the camel-road, passing from herbage to herbage with many a burning stretch between. And the quern goes with them.

To Celtic women, like their sisters of the desert, the quern was the symbol of toil and ache, of such weariness that it is good to know that it is gone out of use for ever. Yet in the ancient chants, which have come down to us, the beauty of thankfulness still lives on, and still we hear the women singing, as the moonwhite meal fell upon the outspread sheepskin,

> O minding Three,
> Blessed be ye
> For meal that's meat,
> For meal that's life

To labouring man
And fainting wife.
O minding Three,
Blessed be ye
For meal that's wine
And music and grace,
That drives the plough,
And fells the tree,
And builds a joy
In every place.

May the glory of all I am and see and have,
keep thankfulness to Thee warm within my
thought.

THE MILKING-CROON

Directness and simplicity are still the key-notes of Highland faith in God, and if this kind of faith lacks something of the four-squareness of the conviction a man gains by doing battle against doubt and self, yet it yields a fine serenity. God is a friend in all weathers. Whatever is is best. Whatever shall be is purposed. Finding nothing common or unclean, we Highland people sense Divinity everywhere, in opal dawns and quiet seas: in trusty friendship and in cleansing laughter: in food and drink, in glistering fish, or in the flesh of deer. 'We are God's guests,' said a pious man of the Lewis, 'and 'tis He who keeps the generous table.' It is not surprising, therefore, that in a still simpler age the women crooned a heart-blessing and God's blessing on even the frothing milk :

> White foam of milk,
> Be life to me,
> And life to mine
> Who drink thy wine.
> Most sacred Three,

With blessing bend
Over this gift
Your care doth send.
Yea, whoso drinks
Of this white feast,
Gift him with vision
Clear to see
Thy love full-brimmed
Within the cup
Raised to his lips'
Necessity.

Because Thy design for each of us is perfect in its friendliness, may we count nothing strange which befalls us on our journey. Rather may our spirits keep breathing the upland air of trust.

Because Thou makest each today wonderful for body and mind, may we welcome the coming of that eternal and unshadowed day in which we shall see Thy face and know the truth at last.

THE BLESSING OF THE SEED

At Fontenoy, the night before the battle, some veteran soldiers from the glens spoke of the spirit in which a man should face the hazard of war. One said, ' I drink and care not.' Another, 'I hope and yield not.' And still another, 'If I fall, why not? Death's spear shall pierce me at the last.' But he who had seen most and was most valiant said, 'I give myself into Another's keeping, and fear not.' No strangesome word for an Islesman who set forth upon no venture or journey or fishing or hunting or seed-sowing but first asked the blessing of Heaven's King. Surely this is the majesty and crown of faith, that a man does not even the smallest thing save he asks the favour of God. Lovely to think of the farmer bowing before the winnowed corn and chanting :

I will go forth to sow my seeds
In the name of Him whose growth it
    needs,
Friday shall be my chosen day.

And every seed that swooning lies
Beneath the cold of winter's eyes
Shall root take in my clay.

Kissed by the winds that lightsome run
My blades shall leap to meet the sun,
Fast yellowing to each golden ray.

May I feel Thy presence at the heart of my
desire, and so know it for Thy desire for me.
Thus shall I prosper. Thus see that my purpose
is from Thee. Thus have power to do the good
which endures.

THE PRAYER-CHARM

The prayer-charms of the Celt can be traced to the fear of warlock and fairy and witch—a baneful trinity who were invested with a vast power of hurt. Over mind-life, over body-life. Over crops and cattle. Over the health of children. Over one's own prosperity. Against their spells, therefore, he fashioned the prayer-charm, the soul's breastplate and Excalibur.

Some call them incantations, and this may be true in part. But as well as this they are mile-stones upon the road of Faith along which the race moves to God. In the realm of science the higher mind has achieved marvels which seem to wear, at least to all who are reverent, an aureole of wonder. In the realm of spirit may not a higher faith, more eager, more adventurous, and more persistent, win potencies that shall clothe both mind and body with a new greatness and a new divinity.

A PRAYER-CHARM TO BE SAID UPON THE KNEES
IN AN HOUR OF STRONG TEMPTATION

O Holy Christ,
O Lord of Light,
Succour me now
In my affright.

O Holy Christ,
Ride fast and rout
My foes that ring
My soul about.

O Holy Christ,
Now in this hour
Keep tryst with me
And be my tower,
Most Holy Christ.

Deliver me from self-trustfulness. In the
frequent days in which I must do battle with
my self for foe, arm me with a constant trust in
Thee.

THE AGE OF GOLD

If we could draw aside a lap of Time's curtain and, say two centuries ago, find ourselves, upon a wind-fresh morning, in an island haven watching the boats make ready to go, much would we hap on to stir the blood and to still the heart. Laughter and teasing and, like enough, from women some secret tears. Then a call for silence. Then the prayer to be said by all wise men who fare over the breast of the sea :

> Round our skiff be God's aboutness
> Ere she try the deeps of sea,
> Sea-shell frail for all her stoutness
> Unless Thou her Helmsman be.

Rough times were those, to be sure, beset with peril and ill for a man's flesh to bear. None the less, in the matter of a delivering faith in God, they were the age of gold.

❖

I strive to be strong. In spite of all my yesterdays, perfect my hope in Thee.

BEAUTY MADE CAPTIVE

What is the origin of that creative urge which finds its expression in architecture, in music, in painting, in literature? It is not merely the desire to imprison emotion. Rather is it the passion to give truth and beauty a permanent form. But who can achieve this form except through travail of spirit: through forgetfulness of self: along the red road of sacrifice?

The pipe-music of the Gael, hill-sweet and sea-sweet, offers many a proof of this commonplace. In their College of Music at Borreraig the MacCrimmons fasted for two days, Dr. Neil Ross tells us, before composing. Nor, while the vision beckoned, did they yield their eyes to sleep or mouth to speech. To their chosen pupils, heirs of their skill, the MacCrimmons passed on the technique of music. But, as well, a secret more precious by far, which was and is, that whoever plays a coronach must feel the dark woe of it in his own heart: must rejoice in the spring when he pours out a golden tune: must himself throb with courage if he would make its note sound in another's heart. Thus a noble musician like Ian Dall Mackay dared to hope that, though blind, he might translate the seven colours of the rainbow into sound. It fell upon a calm eve that a peerless bow arched the sky. At the same moment, so the tale goes, a skylark rose loud-singing, flooding the silences of glen and ben with her melody. ' Surely,' the blind one whispered softly, ' this is the tune of the rainbow.' And himself caught the glory of it, and made it ours for ever.

I stand in the warm sunshine of this perfect day, my heart a song of praise for this jewel dropped from Thy hand. O Wondrous One, how beautiful must be Thy mind! How deep Thy faith that I must make response. Make me equal to Thy trust. May all this loveliness I see, pass into my spirit, then flow forth again from me into the beauty of right-doing and of love which gives itself.

A RUNE AGAINST ENVY

Though, like the poor, the envious man is with us still, we of today know that envy has no wizardry to do us harm. But in another age the thought of men ran otherwise. For, if the fisher's net were empty and his neighbour's full ; if the white milk were scant of measure ; if the sea-fowler fell from the perilous crag, then envy was at work. So, since another's goodness is buttress to one's own, the prudent hied them to a holy man, one who had power over ill and the rune that was shield against the onset of covetry. Such a one as :

> Whoso wishes
> Thee ill, not good,
> Grudging thee store
> Of wine or food,
> Thy winnowed corn,
> Thy flesh of deer
> Thyself did'st kill
> To make thee cheer,
> May God between
> Him stand and thee !
> God foil his hate !

> And may the sea
> His wishes drown!
> Of hurt to thee,
> Yea, all his spells
> Clean dissipate !

Three centuries later, truth and knowledge for his armour, a mystic Islesman said, ' I am a freeman in a world of law. And who can harm me if I mean, speak, and do well.' A noble thought. The sun has broken through the cloud.

Confer Thy greatness on me. Share with me the essence of Thy spirit. Dower me with such a splendour of mind that I shall be able to rejoice in another's good, in another's joy.

O Christ, my King, for this fair earth which is my home a while, I bow my knee: for dreaming isles: for quickening dawns: for still noons: for the laughter of children: for love in lovers' eyes. Yet my joy is sevenfold, since every sound and sight is a voice that tells of Thee. I

on the white rose, and lo! Thy heart is
I hear the hill-burn whisper that Thy
r me outlasts his flowing. And the rain
y tears whenever I wound Thy dream of
me. And the sun is the shining of Thy face at
every victory. I win for the spirit of Thy
gentleness and truth.

THE END